Go Wild!
WILDLIFE DESIGNS TO COLOR

KELLY MONTGOMERY

Note

Welcome to the funny farm! Here you'll find everything from a spotted gorilla to a checkered zebra and a buffalo donning paisley-printed fur. This zany menagerie features thirty illustrations of some of the wackiest wildlife you've ever seen. Just use your imagination and color these designs any way you like!

Bibliographical Note

Go Wild! Wildlife Designs to Color is a new work, first published by Dover Publications, Inc., in 2012.

International Standard Book Number
ISBN-13: 978-0-486-48126-5
ISBN-10: 0-486-48126-3

Manufactured in the United States by Courier Corporation
48126301
www.doverpublications.com

4

9

16

25